TRAITS OF A JACKASS MANAGER

A How-Not-To Guide for Managers Old and New

CHARLES A. SENNEWALD

ELSEVIER

AMSTERDAM • BOSTON • HEIDELBERG • LONDON
NEW YORK • OXFORD • PARIS • SAN DIEGO
SAN FRANCISCO • SINGAPORE • SYDNEY • TOKYO

Butterworth-Heinemann is an imprint of Elsevier

B
H

Butterworth-Heinemann is an imprint of Elsevier
225 Wyman Street, Waltham, MA 02451, USA
The Boulevard, Langford Lane, Kidlington, Oxford, OX5 1GB, UK

First published 2012.

Notices
Knowledge and best practice in this field are constantly changing. As new research and
experience broaden our understanding, changes in research methods, professional
practices, or medical treatment may become necessary.

Practitioners and researchers must always rely on their own experience and
knowledge in evaluating and using any information, methods, compounds, or
experiments described herein. In using such information or methods they should be
mindful of their own safety and the safety of others, including parties for whom they
have a professional responsibility.

To the fullest extent of the law, neither the Publisher nor the authors, contributors, or
editors, assume any liability for any injury and/or damage to persons or property as a
matter of products liability, negligence or otherwise, or from any use or operation of
any methods, products, instructions, or ideas contained in the material herein.

Library of Congress Cataloging-in-Publication Data
A catalog record for this book is available from the Library of Congress

British Library Cataloguing in Publication Data
A catalogue record for this book is available from the British Library

ISBN: 978-0-12-397197-5

For information on all Butterworth-Heinemann publications
visit our website at *www.elsevierdirect.com*

Typeset by: diacriTech, India

This book has been manufactured using Print On Demand technology. Each copy is
produced to order and is limited to black ink. The online version of this book will show
color figures where appropriate.

OUTLINE

Thank you, HS.

The management process of achieving organizational goals by working with and through other people is as much an art as a science. Those in leadership roles, irrespective of the level of responsibility, affect the lives of every employee who reports to him or her in both subtle and dramatic ways – far more than many leaders suspect. What a manager says or does not say, or does or does not do, is highly visible to employees and is often carefully scrutinized. Flaws as well as strengths in one's management style tend to be exaggerated. By virtue of the manager–employee relationship, an exaggerated flaw can dominate and overshadow or otherwise neutralize good qualities.

Because we are all human, a managerial blunder committed in ignorance is forgivable. Theoretically, once the error is recognized, the manager will work to correct it. However, there are those who understand their past (and present) mistakes, yet, for whatever reasons, persist in exhibiting these known flaws in their daily managerial style. These flaws then become entrenched and hereinafter are referred to as "jackass management traits."

It only stands to reason that employees who are resentful, disgusted, or disappointed; who feel cheated, underappreciated, ignored, or abused; or who are angry with their supervisors for any number of reasons are not going to do their best. Employees, who have a poor perception of their supervisor, and the employer are not going to perform as well as those who feel valued. This appears to be true in a wide variety of industries and at all levels of the supervisor–employee relationship. It behooves every supervisor to eradicate jackass management traits within their organization and to start by being an example to others. Knowing the managerial pitfalls – or jackass traits – is the first step in learning how to avoid them.

The Manager Who Seeks to be "Liked" Rather than Respected

Everyone wants to be liked; it is part of human nature. Being liked gives us confidence and a sense of well-being. However, the manager who strives to be "one of the gang," or wants to be liked by everyone, gets trapped into trying to please everyone by avoiding unpopular decisions or ignoring disciplinary problems. Generally,

■ **FIGURE 1-1 The Popularity Kid.**

people prefer to work in a well-ordered environment. They do not really want their supervisor to always focus on being a nice person if it means sacrificing fairness or integrity. The managers who avoid saying "no" or "don't" simply make the workload more difficult for everyone else. Employees are not necessarily looking for a buddy in their supervisor. Most of them know that too much socializing can lead to a compromised leader. What they do look for is a fair, impartial, predictable, honest administrator or leader who sets, practices, and maintains standards. Those qualities gain respect, which is far more important in leadership than being liked (Fig. 1-1).

The Manager Who Ignores the Opinions and Advice of Employees

Also known as the "know-it-all," one wonders if this type of supervisor really believes they know it all; or if such a manager is actually insecure and is fearful of employees discovering that he or she does not have all the answers all the time. There is nothing wrong with not having all the answers all the time. In fact, there is nothing wrong with being honest and saying, "I don't know."

What really motivates and encourages many employees is to be asked, by their supervisor, "What do you think?" They think plenty! It is amazing how many smart people there are, and it is equally amazing what they can do in terms of solving problems and coming up with creative strategies and ideas. To ask individuals such questions as, "What do you think?"; "What are we doing that we shouldn't be doing?"; and "What are we not doing that we should be doing?" invariably brings out rich food for thought. To deny oneself and one's organization that input is akin to operating with one arm tied behind the back. After all, the collective wisdom of the group or department surely exceeds that of even the most brilliant managers.

The manager who can create the climate in which employees have some voice in the things that happen and in which they participate or somehow contribute to the operation as team members will get the most out of employees. They will feel that they are part of the team and therefore will want the team to succeed. And a successful team reflects favorably on its leader! (Fig. 1-2).

■ **FIGURE 1-2 The Know-It-All.**

The Manager Who Fails to Delegate Properly

The true art of delegation includes giving responsibility with commensurate authority and then holding the employee accountable for his or her use of that authority. The primary mistake made by managers when delegating is that they give an employee a task (responsibility) but fail to give the necessary authority to discharge that task. Put another way, the manager keeps strings attached to the assignment in terms of insisting it be done his or her way, not the employee's way, and reserves for himself the final (as well as many intermediate) decisions, acting as "judge" (and jury!) on all issues.

Two key conditions develop with this managerial flaw: (1) the manager becomes mired down in nitpicking relatively unimportant decisions, which creates a bottleneck in the process and undermines the whole point of delegation and (2) employees lose "heart" because they know that their supervisor may arbitrarily override their plans and decisions in favor of their own. They say, "What's the difference what I do? He'll change it anyhow." Not only is it demoralizing, but it's a poor use of both managerial and employee time and a waste of the potential talent of all parties (Fig. 1-3).

■ FIGURE 1-3 The Judge.

The Manager Who Ignores the Training and Developmental Needs of Employees

This is the manager who attends his or her favorite training courses, seminars, and conventions but would not dream of spending the money to send employees. Often, this supervisor knows most of the information and data that will be presented at a seminar, so he or she attends primarily for the networking opportunities. The pity is, employees could learn a great deal from these trainings, even if the supervisor cannot! However, he or she cannot always seem to find the funds for employees to attend trainings or feels that other demands of the organization have priority. This is the same supervisor who might resent the training department's request or requirement that the staff attend company-sponsored programs because their attendance at these programs takes time away from the job.

Employees with potential and ambition thirst for education and training to help them grow. Denying them that opportunity stunts their growth, stifles their potential, fails to maximize their latent talents, and creates resentment. After all is said and done, the greatest resource any organization has is its people. Unfortunately, this type of supervisor is not sensitive to that (Fig. 1-4).

■ FIGURE 1-4 The Stifler.

The Manager Who Insists on Doing Everything "The Company Way"

Some have cynically said that there are three ways to do a task: (1) the right way, (2) the wrong way, and (3) the company way. There really is a fourth: a better way.

The manager who is a stickler for compliance with doing things "by the book" (the company way) as though it were a holy tablet, and who is more concerned about the means than the end result is the one who blocks enthusiasm, interest, creativity, and motivation. Some flexibility in standard procedures on the part of the supervisor might result in reduced costs and increased production. This kind of manager, who is compliance oriented and avoids risks, typifies the person who has peaked out career-wise. He or she may very well not want to "rock the boat" in an effort to maintain their current position (Fig. 1-5).

■ FIGURE 1-5 Moses.

The Manager Who Fails to Give Credit When Credit Is Due

Nothing is more deflating, disappointing, or demotivating than having a supervisor ignore or overlook an achievement. A sincere "Job well done" or "Thank you" goes a long way. A note or brief memo from the supervisor expressing appreciation for a task well done is valued by employees. Even a desk-side or hallway expression of thanks means a great deal. Thoughtlessness can be perceived as disinterest or dissatisfaction on the supervisor's part. Interestingly, the supervisor who appears to be blind to achievement more often than not is the same supervisor who easily recognizes mistakes. Slow to praise, quick to criticize. Everyone can spot this "jackass trait" a mile away. People expect praise and recognition when it is earned and accept constructive criticism when it is due.

A supervisor who fails to credit good work might be viewed as stingy or miserly with their praise. This same supervisor may also fail to promote employees or grant deserved salary increases (Fig. 1-6).

■ FIGURE 1-6 The Miser.

The Manager Who Treats Employees as Subordinates

Employees are people first and employees second. Each person is the center of his or her own universe. Gather a group of employees in a room and ask them who in the room is the most important person. They will likely each be thinking, "I am." And rightly so.

The manager who looks down on or treats employees as inferiors, intentionally or not, threatens their very sense of self-esteem. This attitude can lead to resentment by the employees and foster bickering, gossip, and an unmotivated staff. Employees will likely stay at their job out of necessity, but not give it their all – their potential, their energy, or their loyalty. Rather, they will simply show up to do the work at hand, without being invested in the organization (Fig. 1-7).

■ FIGURE 1-7 The Snob.

The Manager Who Ignores Employees' Complaints

Not listening is a luxury which only jackasses and dictators can afford. How many companies today are unionized because employees' complaints went unheeded? Employees do not necessarily vote for unions, they vote against management. Employees are easily frustrated by management that ignores their problems, real or imaginary. They want their concerns – whatever they are – to be heard by management.

Not only should a manager listen, he or she should find ways to encourage employees to get things off their chests, to point out unfair practices, and to complain about anything from dirty restrooms or poor cafeteria food to feeling overworked or underappreciated. Long gone are the days when employees stoically accepted what management had to offer. The supervisor who ignores employees' complaints today is the kind of jackass that should have been put out to pasture years ago (Fig. 1-8).

■ FIGURE 1-8 The Deaf (and Dumb).

The Manager Who Does Not Keep People Informed

Whenever you hear employees say, "You never know what's going on around here," you have a problem. Ideally, employees should not have to ask the question "Why?" because the question should have been answered before it was even asked. People spend more of their waking hours on the job than at home or anywhere else. It is a big and an important part of their lives. It is big for their families, too, because the job puts food on the table, pays the rent, buys a vehicle, provides medical insurance, and so forth.

Therefore, everything that happens on the job is important and is scrutinized with keen interest. When someone is transferred, promoted, resigns, retires, comes aboard, goes on medical or family leave, or is laid off, in one way or another, it affects someone else. The same is true of organizational realignments, benefit changes, and new shifts or hours. These changes should be explained to all the employees at the earliest possible time.

■ FIGURE 1-9 The Secret Agent.

Usually, an official notice is sent around, but often the distribution system is sluggish or those in the know leak the news and it gets distorted. On top of that, depending on the kind of communication system in use at the company, many news items do not even reach all employees. The news is known to supervisors or managers who are supposed to inform their staff, but fail to.

To further magnify the frustration, you find the "secret agent jackasses" whose philosophy is, "Don't tell anyone unless there is a need to know," thus shrouding in mystery any changes and activities within their own departments (Fig. 1-9).

The problem with poor communication, or no communication, is that it breeds suspicion among the troops, and frequently more time is spent speculating over changes than is spent on the work itself.

The Manager Who Holds His or Her Assistant Back

Every supervisor should be developing his or her "backup employee" or assistant (often an assistant manager) to take over the supervisor's job, as soon as possible. At the same time, that manager should be preparing for a higher level of responsibility in or out of the present structure. Most employees want to move up the organizational ladder, and the effective supervisor fosters this healthy "bubbling-up" climate.

Generally, there are two types of managers: one has the desire and ability to move up, whereas the other has no desire and/or ability to move up. In the latter case, it is grossly unfair to keep a promising employee from advancing somewhere else in the company just to have a backup in one's own office in the event of an emergency, such as a heart attack or sudden illness. The end result in such circumstances is that the employee, who is obviously talented enough to make the assistant manager level, in due time will see that he or she is being kept on ice for emergency reasons and will simply leave the company for opportunities elsewhere. The company loses a valuable resource and an expensive investment (Fig. 1-10).

■ FIGURE 1-10 The Jailer.

The Manager Who Views the Disciplinary Process as a Punitive Action

Punishment is not good discipline. In fact, it is the worst form of discipline because it is negative in nature. Regrettably, many managers equate discipline with punishment, and they are off base.

The word *discipline* is derived from the Latin term *discipulus*, which means "learning." Today, when understood and seen as a constructive tool, discipline means the training that corrects, molds, or strengthens an employee in the interests of achieving organizational goals. Punishment comes after all else fails. Punishment should be a means to an end that should be organizational, not personal.

Here is a way of looking at discipline that you should never forget: the effective disciplinary process condemns the act, not the person. The approach is, "You are OK, but what you did is not OK." By focusing on the performance (or performance failure) rather than the

■ FIGURE 1-11 The Whipper.

person, the whole process takes on a constructive dimension and is palatable to everyone. The manager who condemns or attacks the person instead of the person's performance consequently is not going to get satisfactory results. That manager is doing things backward, which suggests that perhaps the manager has a thick skull – similar to that of a jackass (Fig. 1-11).

The Manager Who Fails to Back Up His or Her Staff

What a way to lose the support and respect of employees – hang them out to dry when something goes amiss! Employees under this supervisor know where they stand when trouble rears its ugly head. They stand alone, because the supervisor disassociates himself or herself from anything that goes wrong. After washing their hands of any guilt, he or she attempts to fix the blame on someone else (also known as throwing someone "under the bus"), rather than fixing the problem.

■ FIGURE 1-12 The Coward.

This fair-weather manager has an insatiable appetite for organizational successes – achieved, of course, by other employees. He or she accepts full honor and glory for all the good things, even while letting shine forth a noble hint of modesty. This manager is indeed a winner. Never makes an error and takes all the credit. This jackass actually has the traits of a pig (Fig. 1-12).

The Manager Whose Word Cannot Be Trusted

The "pretender" is a slippery character with an almost uncanny ability to cloud up issues and renege on earlier promises or statements. Employees are likely to walk out of the office confused and baffled after a session with this kind of manager. An employee may walk into that office to inquire about a promised early performance review (with a possible increase), but the manager pretends as if he or she is confused

■ FIGURE 1-13 The Pretender.

about any earlier promise and then suggests that the employee must be the one who is confused. This kind of supervisor may very well have a sign on the wall that reads: "I know you believe you understand what you think I said, but I am not sure you realize that what you heard is not what I meant."

Talk about tragedy. This kind of manager loves the pretender style and somehow believes that the style contributes to the overall success of the organization. The truth is that this manager is viewed with suspicion and disdain, not only as a manager of people but also as a human being. What a frustrating work climate this manager creates! (Fig. 1-13).

The Manager Who Avoids Making Decisions

Nothing can be quite as exasperating as waiting for a supervisor to make a decision. If a project poses a critical question, the entire project remains motionless until the decision is made. Nothing happens.

Some flaws in management styles never leak beyond a given department, but this particular flaw has a way of becoming widely known, snickered over, and causing exasperation. This is true because sooner or later "Ol' Undecided" will be faced with a decision that will affect the entire company and not just his or her department.

■ FIGURE 1-14 The Undecided.

How many times has the following occurred? Employee A asks employee B, "What's the status on the new proposal you want approved?" Employee B answers, "It's sitting on Harry's (The Undecided) desk." And there it will stay for quite some time.

Unwillingness to make decisions clearly reflects a lack of self-confidence or fear of making the wrong decision (an error!). A key leadership responsibility is to give direction. Decisions give direction. Failure to act, let alone act in a timely fashion, is a serious deficiency that breeds frustration and a "don't-give-a-damn" attitude among employees (Fig. 1-14).

The Manager Who "Plays Favorites"

Showing partiality to one or more employees at the expense of others, always favoring one employee's ideas over all others, or bestowing bonuses or promotions on a select few quickly generates hostility toward the "favored" and resentment against the manager. Supervisors have no choice but to work among their staff in an objective, impartial manner. Anything less than that is blatantly unfair. It causes problems in institutions such as schools, government, and the home. It invariably leads to organizational disharmony.

■ FIGURE 1-15 The Bestower.

A manager may well harbor personal likes and dislikes for various employees, but if he or she has any class or a sense of professionalism, no one will ever know (Fig. 1-15).

The Manager Who Fails to Stay Current in the Field

Keeping up with the "state of the art" in terms of new technology; new concepts; new studies; changing laws; and changing attitudes, trends, and needs is a personal as well as professional requirement, especially for those in leadership roles. To discover that a supervisor is "behind the times" or is not tech savvy is a source of wonderment and frustration to employees, one that ultimately leads to a credibility gap. There is no way to bridge that gap once it has developed, except of course to become current. It is as though the supervisor has become Rip van Winkle and slept while the world changed around them. Catching up is an awesome

■ FIGURE 1-16 Rip Van Winkle.

task when one considers that one of the reasons behind the need to catch up is that the manager is too lazy to stay current. That very laziness is like a disease that accelerates in its crippling growth. Reversal is rare.

A manager cannot just reach the top of any given plateau and rest on the laurels of that accomplishment. If you do not grow vertically then at least grow horizontally; that is, stay abreast of your business, keep learning, keep improving, and keep growing.

Absolutely nothing remains constant or static, except the intellect of a jackass (Fig. 1-16).

The Manager Who Enjoys "Pouring on" More Work than an Employee Can Handle

No useful purpose is served by inundating employees with more work than they can handle. Invariably quality is sacrificed for quantity, and desperation over too much to do in too little time leads to compromises that can include deception and destruction of assignments. Most people enjoy their work and find satisfaction in the achievement of a job well done. To purposely overload employees "just to be sure they are kept busy" directly contributes to high turnover, mental fatigue, some physical disabilities with resultant lost time, and general resentment and frustration. This type of supervisor might categorize those who stay home ill as malingerers and those who object to the way work is assigned as "lazy." The manger is so dedicated to getting the maximum work out of every employee, that coffee breaks, lunch breaks, holidays, and vacation breaks are resented. This jackass is happiest when people come in early, work late, and come in on their day off when such extra time is off-the-record and without compensation.

Only a jackass is blind to the fact that maximum production and organizational efficiency come from employees who enjoy their work and produce willingly (Fig. 1-17).

■ FIGURE 1-17 The Slave Driver.

The Manager Who Acts or Overreacts Too Quickly

This manager would be dangerous if armed – leaping before looking, acting before thinking, and shooting without aiming (always from the hip). Making on-the-spot decisions without the facts is another characteristic of this kind of manager. This supervisor also changes employees' plans without the benefit of discussion. Those who are in charge of executing the manager's plans are never given any notice if the plans are changed. This managerial type reacts to normal problems as though they were crises. When the smoke clears, others are blamed for the mess this supervisor caused.

People resent taking the blame or being criticized for conditions created by their supervisor. That leads to secrecy and an overall "pass the buck" attitude. Supervisors cannot react to something unknown, so at times employees may try to tackle issues or change

■ FIGURE 1-18 Hair-trigger Harry.

direction without their supervisor knowing. What a breakdown in communications! The result is that this "jackass" becomes suspicious, goes on the prowl, and in the end reacts that much more irrationally. It becomes a vicious cycle that causes an unhealthy work environment (Fig. 1-18).

The Newly Promoted Manager Who Believes His or Her Manure Is Odorless

Now that this "jackass" received a promotion and is taking over the department, his or her attitude is that everything will now be okay. All the problems are in the past. All the earlier failures will be corrected. Everything will be changed for the better. How poor everything was before. The new manager arrives like a lifeguard ready to save everyone or a knight in shining armor who is going to "clean house" and get this organization on its feet and moving forward again.

Talk about a dumb jackass. This new supervisor does not realize that a lot of people were quite happy with their old supervisor (who they were sorry to see go but pleased about the promotion) and honestly believed that the department had been doing an effective job before the change. Even if an effective job was not being done, only a jackass would come in and make a lot of noise about how bad things have been. It only serves to alienate the staff and create a negative environment.

Newly appointed managers should heed the warning given to children when taught how to cross the street: stop, look, and listen.

Who is to blame for this kind of jackass? The supervisor's own ego as well as his or her boss! That boss probably failed to prepare the new manager for this new venture, this new level of responsibility. Sometimes promotions create giant egos, leaving anyone giddy from the rapid elevation. The new manager believes that he or she must be the best and the only one to save the sinking ship, whether the ship is sinking or not. But in reality, if anyone is in deep – and hot – water, it will be the newly promoted manager. However, with such a swelled head, the new supervisor probably will not go under (Fig. 1-19).

■ **FIGURE 1-19 The Lifeguard.**

The Manager Who Is Moody

Everyone who works for this supervisor speculates, on a daily basis, what kind of mood he or she will be in today. Those who indulge in moodiness tend to have a fascinating array of personalities: cheerful, mean, silly, argumentative, sullen, aggressive, charitable, condescending, and magnanimous, to name a few. Sometimes the same mood will last for 2 consecutive days, which of course prompts a great deal of discussion among employees. The key to all activity in a given day is determining the supervisor's mood. Sometimes employees rely on the supervisor's assistant to interpret the boss's mood.

This managerial style does not breed respect; it breeds cynical disdain for those who indulge in the usurpation of authority. Managers must be predictable and consistent. They should be available to advise, counsel, assist, and work with all employees when the need surfaces. The very idea of having to throw your hat into the office to see if it will be stomped flat and thrown back out, or if you are welcome to enter, is juvenile. Perhaps this is an immature jackass (Fig. 1-20).

■ FIGURE 1-20 Ol' Unpredictable.

Managers Who Fail to Plan and Put Priorities on Their Work

The difference between a fire chief and a firefighter is that the former directs the efforts of the firefighters who make up the company or battalion and the firefighter extinguishes the flames. When you hear a manager say, "All I did today is to put out fires," that tells you the manager abrogated his or her authority as a leader and inserted themselves into the line activity of the organization. Of course, there are occasions when absolutely everyone must pitch in to get a job done, but jackass fire chiefs are consistently in the smoke.

There are several explanations for this. First, the supervisor failed to plan their day's activities and/or failed to stick to the plan. Second, they either failed to put priorities on their work (first things first, etc.) or did not know how to identify their tasks in descending order of importance and then attack those tasks. Third, they find problems surfacing that they choose not to delegate (and delegation is the key to good management) and get in there to resolve the problems themselves. Fourth, they are comfortable with and love fires and putting them out. Fifth, if they did delegate, they did not do so properly – by instilling their staff with the confidence to handle problems – and feel the need to constantly look over the shoulders of their employees.

There are four problems with these managers: (1) they are not properly managing – that is, they are not getting the job done through others; (2) they are not discharging their responsibility to plan, organize, budget, control, direct, staff, and delegate; (3) subordinates are denied the opportunity to perform; and (4) they are not available as leaders because they are up to their shins in cinders.

The need for managers to be available to employees cannot be overstressed. Employees look for, expect, and need leadership. If employees need assistance or advice or have work or personal

■ FIGURE 1-21 The Firefighter.

problems, and their supervisor is not in, where do they go? They go into a state of frustration, that is, where they go! Not to mention decreased confidence in their boss (Fig. 1-21).

The Manager Who Lacks Emotion and Empathy

If you reflect back over the years you can probably recall the person who you would designate as "The Best Boss I Ever Worked For." Everyone has one. You can also recall "The Worst Boss I Ever Worked For." Everyone has one of those too. The difference between the two is often that one was warm and sensitive, nurtured your career, truly cared about you as a person, and showed great confidence in you, and the other may have been cold, indifferent, and cared less about you. For which of these two supervisors did you perform better?

With respect to the poor manager, is it true you harbored some resentment against senior management for supporting such a manager, a manager with a mechanical heart? The interrelationship between people is a very dynamic and emotional process. The jackass that functions like an inanimate robot turns people off emotionally. An organization is not a chart with blocks, lines, department names, and ranks. It is comprised of people – people with human needs and feelings. On the job a primary feeling is one of the selfworth. This need for self-worth spans the entire organization from the chief executive officer to the lowest paid, entry-level position. The manager who is sensitive to that value of worth, who genuinely is concerned about each employee, evokes a reciprocal feeling – as does the unemotional, cold, oblivious manager.

Regrettably, too many managers are simply sharp technicians. They excel in understanding the workers' tasks and tools. Good managers understand and excel (or at least try) in dealing with people who perform the tasks, use the tools, and bring profitability to the enterprise (Fig. 1-22).

■ FIGURE 1-22 The Robot.

The Manager Who Hires Relatives into the Organization

To bring members of one's family into the organization is a no-win situation for everyone. Such family members are not fully accepted by the staff. Employees feel, right or wrong, that relatives have an unfair advantage, and a supervisor's decisions on every aspect of internal affairs that affects relatives is viewed with suspicion and criticism. That is why many enlightened organizations prohibit this practice.

Why are family members not accepted by the staff? There are three reasons: (1) as a rule, employees resent others getting a job through "connection," (2) most employees refuse to believe that relatives who are promoted earned that promotion, and (3) most employees suspect relatives are a "pipeline" and funnel information to the boss. The end result is employees are resentful and guarded.

Only a jackass would opt for the problems incurred when hiring relatives (Fig. 1-23).

■ FIGURE 1-23 Nepotist.

The Manager Who Does Not Treat Women as Equals

This jackass is from a herd that is slowly dwindling but is not yet extinct! It is absolutely archaic to believe that women are unequal to men in the boardroom or in any aspect of business. Gender has nothing to do with one's intellectual capacity, leadership potential, or administrative and executive skills. Discriminating on the basis of sex is a hangover from a society and culture now in the distant past. Today we are in a fast-moving, highly technical, computer-oriented, sophisticated business and industrial era in which pure talent should be the only criteria for advancement into positions of greater responsibility.

More women than ever before are in the work force. In many industries, the percentage of women to men is significant. What a marvelous pool of talent! Only a jackass would purposefully kindle discontentment and resentment in the workplace by engaging in

■ FIGURE 1-24 The Chauvinist.

sexual discrimination. The mainstream of commerce today is maximizing those human resources represented in the female workforce. This jackass is not in the mainstream and will soon become a relic of the past (Fig. 1-24).

The Manager Who Faithfully Practices the Art of Pessimism

This manager sleeps under a wet blanket and throws cold water on every innovative, creative, new, or different idea or strategy. Consistently pat answers include: "We can't." "It won't work." "We tried that before and it didn't work." "No way!" "We can't afford it." "Management won't buy it." "It's not in the budget." "Too risky." "We're not ready for it." "Let's not make any waves." "Don't rock the boat." And, of course, "No."

This manager is flawless in terms of predictability and is unequivocally insurmountable. Enthusiasm within the department is effectively blocked, causing creative employees to grind their teeth in resentful frustration. Employees just marvel at how this "loser" holds the seat of power. "Ol' Negative" is also pessimistic about future plans, the future of the company, the skills of subordinates, and possibly even the future of the country. Worse yet, this pessimism is contagious. Just 10 minutes around Ol' Negative and you are

■ **FIGURE 1-25 OI' Negative.**

depressed too. That is why this manager is avoided like a jackass afflicted with the plague (Fig. 1-25).

The Manager Who Steals Employees' Ideas

The following is a four-act play. As the curtain opens on Act I, Mary Clark, an employee, is seated in front of her supervisor's desk. She is talking with her supervisor, Harry the Pirate. "Harry," she says, "I have what I think could be a dynamite suggestion for our marketing campaign on the XL4300." Harry is interested and asks Mary to spell out her suggestion. When she is done, Harry says, "Well, let me think about it, Mary. I'll get back to you later. Thanks."

Act II: The curtain opens and we see Harry the Pirate sitting in his boss's office talking to Walt Big. "Walt, I've been giving a lot of thought to our marketing strategy on the XL4300. Let me bounce this idea off you, for your reaction." Harry then reiterates Mary's suggestion. When he is done, Walt says, "Harry, that is a great idea! How long would it take you to flesh it out and formalize it on paper? I want to take it upstairs." Harry, who is now beaming with modesty replies, "You know I'm up to my ears on the Big B project. Tell you what I can do. I'll get

Mary Clark to pull it together. We've talked about it already. I'll have her get it up to you before the day's out. She does good work." "Great," says Walt, unsuspecting of Harry's sleight-of-hand act of theft.

Act III: Mary has been called back into Harry the Pirate's office and Harry is talking to her. "Mary, the more I think about the XL4300 suggestion, the more I'm convinced you should go ahead and formalize it. Drop everything else, pull it together, and take it up to Walt's secretary." "Oh, that's exciting," says Mary, "I'll do it right away," and out she goes, unaware she's been victimized.

Act IV takes place the following day in the employee cafeteria, where Mary is having lunch with two of her coworkers. One says, "I overheard Walt Big's secretary telling someone how the Chairman of the Board came down to Walt's office, all excited about a new marketing strategy that came from Harry." "Why, that wasn't Harry's idea. That was mine!" exclaims Mary, almost in tears. "The use of the word *was*, past tense, is correct, my dear," says her colleague. "It is now Harry's. You do the work and he takes the credit. It's his style, you know!" "That's dishonest," says Mary. All nod in agreement as the lights dim and curtain closes (Fig. 1-26).

■ FIGURE 1-26 The Pirate.

The Manager Whose Style and Authority Are Based on Absolute Power

It is no joke that despots still exist in management circles today. They are formal, officious little dictators. They know best and the employee's role is to do as told without questioning why. One cannot help but think this jackass is indeed playing a role on stage because it is such a contrast to modern practices, but they are still around. They tend to intimidate everyone around them and love to have people speak in hushed tones in their presence, as well as step aside as they move straight ahead. To them the organization is like a supreme "state," and it is their sacred duty to rule with an iron hand. A strategy they share in common with one another is to call employees to their office to make them sit outside, agonizing over why they were called.

In the early twentieth century, such despotism characterized the usual managerial/supervisorial style and was accepted as a way of organizational life. Today, despots are despised with a passion. No one will ever know how much company's loss of productivity can be directly attributed to this strutting jackass (Fig. 1-27).

■ FIGURE 1-27 The Despot.

The Manager Who Seems Oblivious to What Is Happening

Managers of people do not have the freedom to pick and choose what they want and do not want to see. And yet, there are those who seem to have blind spots when it comes to certain acts or people within their department. This visual impairment runs a range from "spots" to "tunnel vision" to "total." If effective and professional managers came on the scene, they would be horrified to find the chaos that occurs when a supervisor chooses not to see unchecked behavior that is not acceptable in the organization. The truth is, if one member of the staff starts "getting away with murder," it becomes common knowledge among the troops and others may follow suit. Many times blindness comes from a fear of taking corrective action – not wanting to be disliked or considered "mean."

■ FIGURE 1-28 The Visually Impaired.

When employees "goof off" it is not because they prefer that conduct over productive work. It is because productive work is not necessarily rewarding in a poorly disciplined environment. Most of us tend to gravitate to where the rewards are. If rewards do not come from their supervisor but come from peers instead, then those are the rewards that are sought. Lone workers who keep their nose to the grindstone in this kind of workplace will probably be ridiculed. Better to be rewarded than ridiculed, right? If you can get away with surfing the Internet all day or bringing home company supplies, what else can you get away with? (Fig. 1-28).

The Manager Who Loves to "Sack" Employees

Unfortunately, there are those jackasses that take absolute delight in firing employees. They will diligently monitor a likely prospect, allowing correctable failures to mount and accumulate, so that the killing blow will not be deflected by some human resource representative or otherwise rational executive. When that prospect receives walking papers, the headhunter goes about, unproductively, selecting a new victim. One suspects these managers notch the edge of the desk with each "kill" (little notches if on probation, big notches if past probation).

The truth is that it is relatively easy to terminate someone compared to working with a marginal employee and salvaging the initial investment that goes into the recruiting, selecting, processing, orienting, and training. Most employees are salvageable and want constructive criticism and guidance to achieve acceptable company standards.

Headhunters are easy to spot because they tend to sneak about, noting mistakes, and eyeing weaknesses. Although they are loathed, they wear the mantle proudly because they perceive their mission as one of purging the impure from the organization. The tragedy here is that some fall victim to this jackass and their termination is unfair. When managers and organizations are perceived as "unfair," the variety and magnitude of subsequent consequences can be costly (Fig. 1-29).

■ FIGURE 1-29 The Headhunter.

The Manager Who Embarrasses Subordinates in the Presence of Others

Discipline, corrective action, constructive criticism, or reprimands constitute a necessary and ongoing activity in every organization. Good managers know when and where to conduct such activity. Jackasses don't! Every employee understands and should expect correction, if warranted. However, they have natural expectations as to how, when, and where that correction will take place. If handled in the privacy of an office, in the context of a discussion about performance (or nonperformance) rather than a personal attack, more often than not the employee will listen to what is said and correct the questionable performance.

However, employees who are tongue-lashed, shouted at, or are "chewed out" in the presence or earshot of others are embarrassed and humiliated. They focus and dwell on the humiliating experience. They profit or learn nothing constructive or positive from the correction but rather shift guilt, as it were, from their performance to the equally wrongful performance of the humiliator. Not only does the victim harbor resentment, but peers who witnessed the public

WHAT A STUPID MISTAKE!

■ FIGURE 1-30 The Humiliator.

display identify with the victim, and they too harbor rejection and resentment against the boss.

All this to what good end? None – there is no good in this behavior! (Fig. 1-30).

The Manager Who Follows "Double Standards" in the Organization

A key responsibility of every manager is to set a proper example. If the work day begins at 9:00 A.M., the manager should be there at 9:00 A.M. Rules that apply to the staff should apply to their supervisor as well. If employees are entitled to purchase company goods, products, or services at a discount, the discount percentage for the boss should be the same, not higher.

If the company allows employees to travel on business via coach and the boss travels with the other employees, he or she too should ride coach and not first class. If the boss must fly first class, then at least that mode of travel should not be flaunted, such as by flying a different carrier or on a different schedule. Certainly rank has its privileges (RHIP). Everyone recognizes that. Privileges in rank are

■ **FIGURE 1-31 Mr. RHIP (Rank Has Its Privileges).**

manifested in salary differences, for example. However, executive salaries are often treated as confidential because the disparity might create resentment. Wisdom and common sense dictate that conspicuous disparities should be avoided.

The jackass managers who flaunt their privileges by parking in restricted areas, coming in late, enjoying long breaks and lunches, going home early, having an assistant do personal business for them, staying in fancier hotels than where their staff stays, and generally relishing their advantages in open view of employees who work shoulder to shoulder with them are inviting problems (Fig. 1-31).

The Manager Who Is a Religious or Racial Bigot

This is a close cousin to the chauvinist who we already identified as a managerial jackass. The difference between the two is the chauvinist simply feels women have limited value, whereas the bigot may be

FIGURE 1-32 The Bigot.

fundamentally opposed to Jews, Protestants, Catholics, Latinos, African Americans, Asians, or other groups. It is simply ridiculous to categorically state that certain classes, groups, or races of people have no executive or managerial potential. A simple jackass may take that position. However, an effective and intelligent leader knows otherwise. Identifying and then maximizing individual talent to achieve organizational goals is a requisite and responsibility of a sound management. I personally could not care less if an individual has a religious conviction, social orientation, or skin pigmentation different from mine. My concern is can this person do the job and do it well?

For just a moment, forget managers denying themselves and the organization the full spectrum of talent present in the greatest resource any firm has – the human resources of its employees – prejudice, be it racial or religious, consistently breeds discontentment and confrontation and this will spill over into organizational life (Fig. 1-32).

Summary

Now we have a grand total of 32 supervisory and managerial flaws found in organizational life. We have chosen to call them jackass management traits. Although it is good to poke fun at some of these otherwise tragic characters, it is sad to consider so many negative traits still existing and, in some cases, prevailing. However, there is a good news. These failings that exist in the very source of our strength and our economic base are rapidly being replaced with a new breed of leadership that understands and appreciates the values of human dignity and worth. This is not coming from the bottom up, but from the top down. There is a growing recognition among senior management that good leadership inspires self-motivation among the troops, rather than harsh or otherwise insensitive managers prodding employees down the jackass trail.

www.ingramcontent.com/pod-product-compliance
Lightning Source LLC
Chambersburg PA
CBHW060514220326
41598CB00025B/3658